Dan and Sam

A Gaelic version of *Dan and Sam*,
entitled *Dan agus Sam*, is also available

First published in 1998 by
SCOTTISH CHILDREN'S PRESS
Unit 14, Leith Walk Business Centre,
130 Leith Walk, Edinburgh EH6 5DT
Tel: 0131 555 5950 • Fax: 0131 555 5018
e-mail: scp@sol.co.uk
http://www.taynet.co.uk/users/scp

Scottish Children's Press is an imprint of Scottish Cultural Press

BRITISH LIBRARY CATALOGUING IN PUBLICATION DATA
A catalogue record for this book is available from the British Library

ISBN: 1 899827 21 8

Printed and bound by Interprint Ltd, Malta

Dan and Sam

Allan Campbell

illustrated by Iain Smith

SCOTTISH CHILDREN'S PRESS

When Dan arrived in our home he was one year old.

He had lived all his life in a city flat, and had never been out in the fresh air.

The first time he was put out in the garden he was so frightened that when a leaf, blown by the wind, passed near him, he ran back into the house.

Dan's fur is white with splashes of black over it.

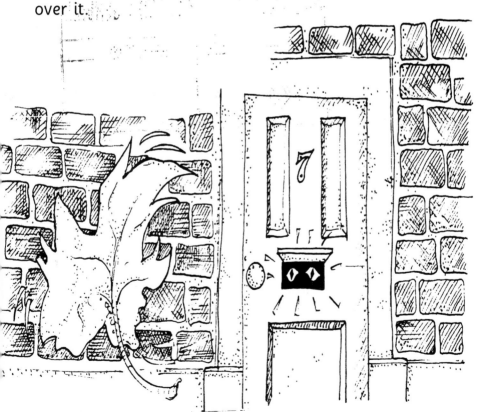

Samantha was a tiny black kitten who was found crying on the street.

She had been abandoned.

She was so tiny that she could sit easily in a hand.

The first thing she did was to have a drink of milk and then walk over to an easy chair.

She just managed to jump up.

She cleaned herself and went off to sleep.

Sam had decided to make her home with us.

So Dan and Sam(antha) came to live with us.

Dan and Sam sleep in a box on the top of the central heating boiler in the garage. On cold winter nights they are always very cosy.

One afternoon, Dan and Sam were playing in the garden.

When it was time for them to have some food they were called to come into the house.

Dan came quickly but, although we called and called, Sam did not appear.

Suddenly, a very faint 'mee-ow' was heard.

It seemed to be coming from a tall poplar tree.

There was wee Sam, up on a branch high above the ground.

She was very frightened. She would not come down.

What could we do? Eventually, by standing on a ladder and holding the head of a soft brush upwards, we found it was just possible to reach Sam.

She was a clever cat and knew what to do.

She jumped on to the brush and was brought down safely.

She never climbed high trees again.

When Dan grew up, he became a big cat. Sam has always remained a small black cat with a white spot on the front of her neck.

In the long summer evenings, Dan and Sam sometimes go for a walk with the family through the woods.

One evening, who did they see coming towards them but Mr Hedgehog, out for his evening walk.

They had never seen such a funny animal before, and ran up to investigate.

Mr Hedgehog was not pleased to see them, and immediately curled up into a ball with all his spikes sticking out.

Dan ran straight into them and got a terrible fright and a sore nose.

Mr Hedgehog stayed curled up until Dan and Sam were far away before starting his walk again.

Hedgehogs always sleep, or hibernate, during the cold winter, usually under a heap of leaves.

One day in December it was unusually warm.

Mr Hedgehog woke up from his deep sleep and decided to leave his snug bed and go for a walk in search of food.

However, it quickly turned cold; then it started raining; and then the snow came.

He became very cold and very hungry and went into the garage where Dan and Sam slept at night.

Hedgehogs should only be fed with meat and never given bread and milk.

Dan and Sam felt very sorry for the poor, cold, shivering Mr Hedgehog.

Dan forgave him for being so prickly and they both allowed him to have some of their cat food.

The next day the weather was better and he returned to his little house under the leaves.

The cat who stays next door is called Jackson.

He is a big black cat and is quite friendly with Dan.

Sam does not like Jackson.

Jackson has a cat flap in the back door of his house, so that he can get in and out of his kitchen when he wishes.

Sam has learned to use this, and whenever she can, she goes in to steal Jackson's food.

Dan is too fat to go through the flap.

We always know when it is going to be a wet day.

Dan and Sam go for only a short walk outside, and then jump up on to the kitchen window to be allowed in.

They try to get into a bedroom so that they can go to sleep.

If they cannot manage this, they lie close to one of the central heating radiators or get into the clothes airing cupboard, which is kept nice and warm by the hot water tank.

In the evenings, when the rain is hitting the windows and the wind is howling outside, Dan and Sam's heaven is lying on the sheepskin rug in front of the fire, sleeping.

In the summer they may lie outside in the shade of a bush, but they prefer to sleep in the conservatory, which is a big glass room built on to the back of the house.

There is a banana tree in the conservatory and its big leaves shade the chair that they sleep on from the hot sun.

When the bananas have ripened, and the tree is removed from the conservatory, we will have to put up a parasol to keep them cool!

Dan and Sam are getting quite old now.

Dan is fourteen and Sam is thirteen years old.

They like to sleep for most of the day; but at nine o'clock each winter evening, if they have been sleeping in front of the fire, they usually wake up, have something to eat and drink, and then go to bed in the garage.

They probably dream of the warm summer days ahead.

Life is very good for Dan and Sam.

Other titles for young readers, available from
SCOTTISH CHILDREN'S PRESS

An A–Z of Scots Words for young readers
1 899827 03 X

Aiken Drum: a story in Scots for young readers
Anne Forsyth; illustrated by Dianne Sutherland; 1 899827 00 5

Bobby Boat and the Big Catch: an Aberdeen Adventure
Thomas Chalmers; illustrated by Billy Dobbie; 1 899827 54 4

Bobby Boat in Trouble at Sea: an Oban Adventure
Thomas Chalmers; illustrated by Billy Dobbie; 1 899827 55 2

Classic Children's Games from Scotland
Kendric Ross; illustrated by John MacKay; 1 899827 12 9

Kitty Bairdie: a story in Scots for young readers
Anne Forsyth; illustrated by Dianne Sutherland; 1 899827 01 3

Moray the Dolphin's Adventure in Loch Ness
Marit Brunskill; illustrated by Craig Ellery; 1 899827 61 7

Rashiecoat: Scots version of Cinderella
Anne Forsyth; illustrated by Dianne Sutherland; 1 899827 19 6

Sandy MacStovie's Monster
Moira Miller; illustrated by Rob Dee; tape available; 1 899827 27 7

Teach the Bairns to Bake: Traditional Scottish Baking for Beginners
Liz Ashworth; 1 899827 24 2

Teach the Bairns to Cook: Traditional Scottish Recipes for Beginners
Liz Ashworth; 1 899827 23 4

Wee Willie Winkie and other rhymes for Scots children
Fiona Petersen (ed.); 1 899827 17 X

When I Wear My Leopard Hat: poems for young children
Dilys Rose; illustrated by Gill Allan; 1 899827 70 6

The Wild Haggis an the Greetin-faced Nyaff
Stuart McHardy; illustrated by Alistair Phimister; 1 899827 04 8

for further information on these or any of our other titles,
please contact SCOTTISH CHILDREN'S PRESS, Unit 14,
Leith Walk Business Centre, 130 Leith Walk, Edinburgh EH6 5DT